Contents

Sounds in this book

a (washing)   augh (taught)   ch (school)
ea (teacher, great)   o (front)   oar (blackboards)
or (word)   ir (shirts)   aw (shawls)

A school trip

Last week my class went to a museum in London. It was called the Ragged School Museum.

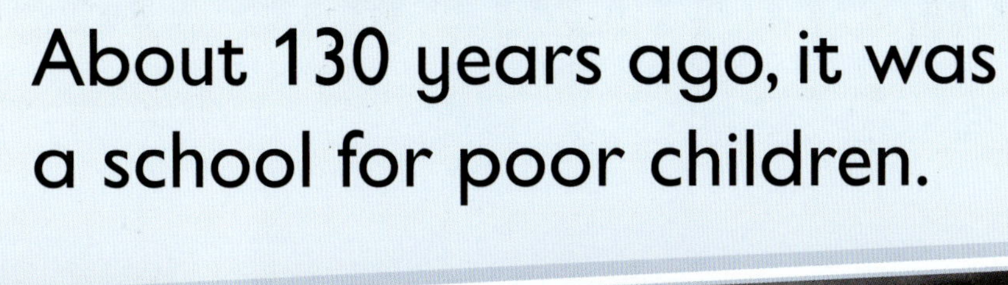

About 130 years ago, it was a school for poor children.

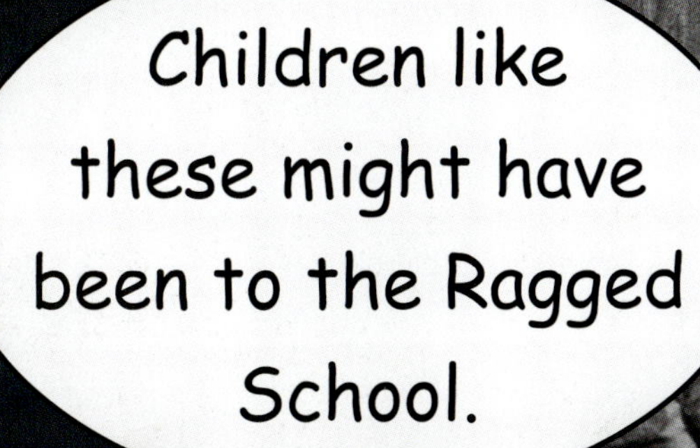

Children like these might have been to the Ragged School.

Children from the past

At the museum, we had to be like children from the past. We were all given old names, like Albert or Betty. We had to put on different clothes, too.

The girls had long skirts and shawls.

The boys had shirts,
waistcoats and caps.

The classroom

First, we were taken to the old classroom. It was full of little wooden desks. The boys sat on one side of the room. The girls sat on the other.

There were two old blackboards at the front of the room. This is where the teacher stood.

Meet Miss Perkins

Then we met our teacher for the day. She was called Miss Perkins. She looked just like teachers did 130 years ago.

Miss Perkins was very strict. First of all, she went round the class and asked to see our hands. She looked at them to check that they were clean!

Looking back

Children were told off if their hands were dirty.

The lesson

Next, Miss Perkins taught us to write. She wrote letters on the blackboard. They were all curly.

We had to copy her letters on little boards. They were made of slate. If any of us said a word, Miss Perkins shouted, "Silence!"

Looking back

Teachers wrote on the blackboard with sticks of chalk.

Time for sums

After that, we did some sums. Miss Perkins wrote a sum on the blackboard. We tried to work it out.

In the past, children were made to wear a dunce's hat if they got sums wrong. One boy, Paul, got to try the hat on.

Sitting up properly

In class, we had to sit up properly. One boy didn't. Miss Perkins made him sit at the front with his arms behind a board.

Another boy kept giggling. Miss Perkins pretended to be very cross with him.
In the past teachers told children off a lot!
15

The old kitchen

When the lesson was over, we visited another room in the museum. It was an old kitchen.

The kitchen had a big black oven called a range. People made a fire in the range. They did their cooking there.

People had coal fires in their houses.

Doing the washing

We found out how people did their washing in the past. They did it in an old tin bath.

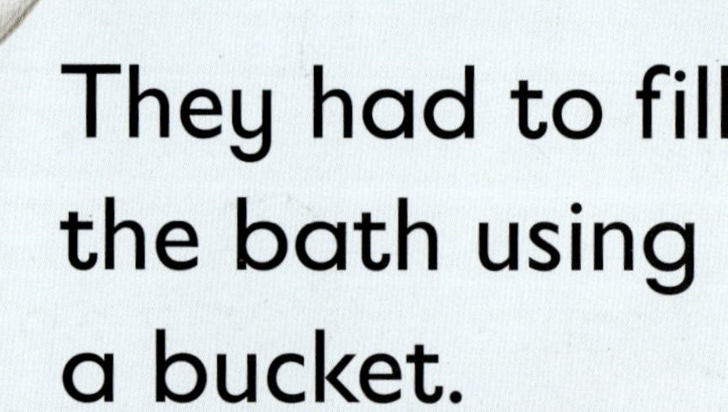

They had to fill the bath using a bucket.

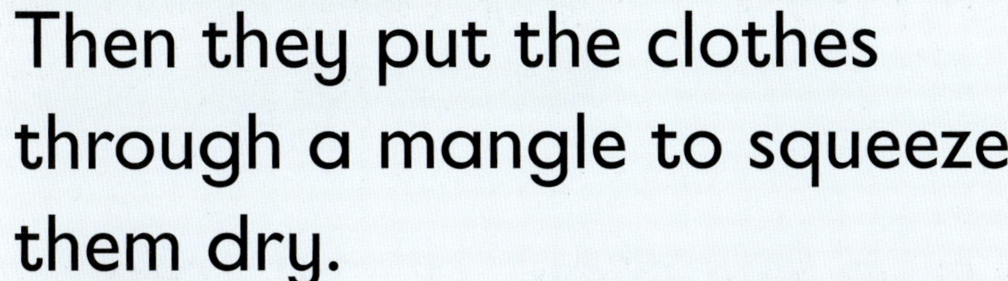

Then they put the clothes through a mangle to squeeze them dry.

Looking back

People did not have hot taps in their houses.

Playtime

We also found out about toys and games in the past. The girls in our class made some little wooden dolls.

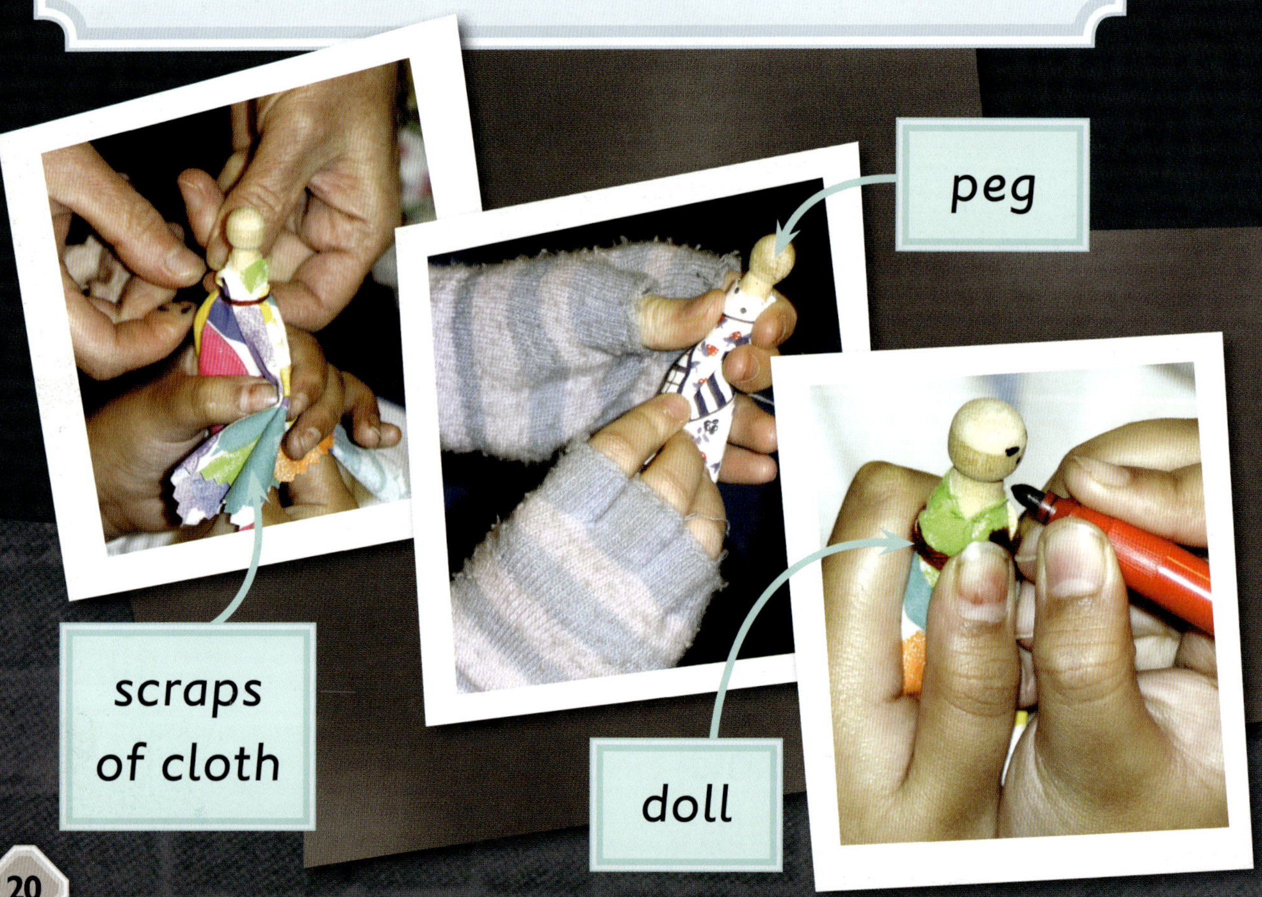

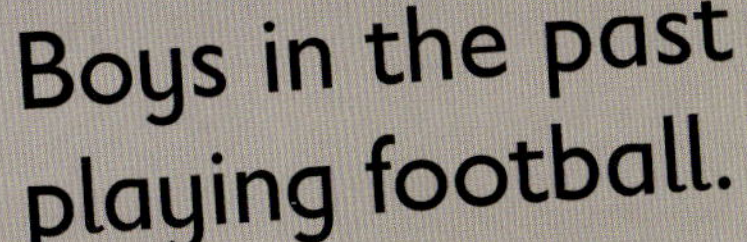

The boys had a game of football.
We made a ball out of a few old
rags. It was all right but not as
good as a real ball.

Time to go home

Then our visit to the Ragged School Museum was over and it was time to leave. We had a great day out!

The Ragged School shut down in 1908. It is a museum now.

I am glad the Ragged School is not my school. I would not like Miss Perkins for my teacher. My teacher is much kinder.

Index